JITTE, HANGETSU, EMPI

BEST KARATE 7

Jitte, Hangetsu, Empi

M. Nakayama

KODANSHA INTERNATIONAL

Tokyo and New York

Front cover photo by Keizō Kaneko; demonstration photos by Yoshinao Murai.

Distributed in the United States by Kodansha International/USA Ltd., 114 Fifth Avenue, New York, New York 10011.

Published by Kodansha International Ltd., 2-2 Otowa 1-chome, Bunkyo-ku, Tokyo 112 and Kodansha International/USA Ltd., 114 Fifth Avenue, New York, New York 10011. Copyright © 1981 by Kodansha International Ltd. All rights reserved. Printed in Japan.

LCC 77-74829
ISBN 0-87011-390-9
ISBN 4-7700-0904-6 (in Japan)

First edition, 1981
Eighth printing, 1989

CONTENTS

Dedicated
to my teacher
GICHIN FUNAKOSHI

The past decade has seen a great increase in the popularity of karate-dō throughout the world. Among those who have been attracted to it are college students and teachers, artists, businessmen and civil servants. It has come to be practiced by policemen and members of Japan's Self-defense Forces. In a number of universities, it has become a compulsory subject, and that number is increasing yearly.

Along with the increase in popularity, there have been certain unfortunate and regrettable interpretations and performances. For one thing, karate has been confused with the so-called Chinese-style boxing, and its relationship with the original Okinawan *Te* has not been sufficiently understood. There are also people who have regarded it as a mere show, in which two men attack each other savagely, or the contestants battle each other as though it were a form of boxing in which the feet are used, or a man shows off by breaking bricks or other hard objects with his head, hand or foot.

If karate is practiced solely as a fighting technique, this is cause for regret. The fundamental techniques have been developed and perfected through long years of study and practice, but to make any effective use of these techniques, the spiritual aspect of this art of self-defense must be recognized and must play the predominant role. It is gratifying to me to see that there are those who understand this, who know that karate-dō is a purely Oriental martial art, and who train with the proper attitude.

To be capable of inflicting devastating damage on an opponent with one blow of the fist or a single kick has indeed been the objective of this ancient Okinawan martial art. But even the practitioners of old placed stronger emphasis on the spiritual side of the art than on the techniques. Training means training of body and spirit, and, above all else, one should treat his opponent courteously and with the proper etiquette. It is not enough to fight with all one's power; the real objective in karate-dō is to do so for the sake of justice.

Gichin Funakoshi, a great master of karate-dō, pointed out repeatedly that the first purpose in pursuing this art is the nurturing of a sublime spirit, a spirit of humility. Simultaneously, power sufficient to destroy a ferocious wild animal with a single blow should be developed. Becoming a true follower of karate-dō is possible only when one attains perfection in these two aspects, the one spiritual, the other physical.

Karate as an art of self-defense and karate as a means of improving and maintaining health has long existed. During the past twenty years, a new activity has been explored and is coming to the fore. This is *sports karate.*

In sports karate, contests are held for the purpose of determining the ability of the participants. This needs emphasizing, for here again there is cause for regret. There is a tendency to place too much emphasis on winning contests, and those who do so neglect the practice of fundamental techniques, opting instead to attempt jiyū kumite at the earliest opportunity.

Emphasis on winning contests cannot help but alter the fundamental techniques a person uses and the practice he engages in. Not only that, it will result in a person's being incapable of executing a strong and effective technique, which, after all, is the unique characteristic of karate-dō. The man who begins jiyū kumite prematurely—without having practiced fundamentals sufficiently—will soon be overtaken by the man who has trained in the basic techniques long and diligently. It is, quite simply, a matter of haste makes waste. There is no alternative to learning and practicing basic techniques and movements step by step, stage by stage.

If karate competitions are to be held, they must be conducted under suitable conditions and in the proper spirit. The desire to win a contest is counterproductive, since it leads to a lack of seriousness in learning the fundamentals. Moreover, aiming for a savage display of strength and power in a contest is totally undesirable. When this happens, courtesy toward the opponent is forgotten, and this is of prime importance in any expression of karate. I believe this matter deserves a great deal of reflection and self-examination by both instructors and students.

To explain the many and complex movements of the body, it has been my desire to present a fully illustrated book with an up-to-date text, based on the experience in this art that I have acquired over a period of forty-six years. This hope is being realized by the publication of the *Best Karate* series, in which earlier writings of mine have been totally revised with the help and encouragement of my readers. This new series explains in detail what karate-dō is in language made as simple as possible, and I sincerely hope that it will be of help to followers of karate-dō. I hope also that karateka in many countries will be able to understand each other better through this series of books.

WHAT KARATE-DŌ IS

Deciding who is the winner and who is the loser is not the ultimate objective. Karate-dō is a martial art for the development of character through training, so that the karateka can surmount any obstacle, tangible or intangible.

Karate-dō is an empty-handed art of self-defense in which the arms and legs are systematically trained and an enemy attacking by surprise can be controlled by a demonstration of strength like that of using actual weapons.

Karate-dō is exercise through which the karateka masters all body movements, such as bending, jumping and balancing, by learning to move limbs and body backward and forward, left and right, up and down, freely and uniformly.

The techniques of karate-dō are well controlled according to the karateka's will power and are directed at the target accurately and spontaneously.

The essence of karate techniques is *kime*. The meaning of *kime* is an explosive attack to the target using the appropriate technique and maximum power in the shortest time possible. (Long ago, there was the expression *ikken hissatsu*, meaning "to kill with one blow," but to assume from this that killing is the objective is dangerous and incorrect. It should be remembered that the karateka of old were able to practice *kime* daily and in dead seriousness by using the makiwara.)

Kime may be accomplished by striking, punching or kicking, but also by blocking. A technique lacking *kime* can never be regarded as true karate, no matter how great the resemblance to karate. A contest is no exception; however, it is against the rules to make contact because of the danger involved.

Sun-dome means to arrest a technique just before contact with the target (one *sun*, about three centimeters). But not carrying a technique through to *kime* is not true karate, so the question is how to reconcile the contradiction between *kime* and *sun-dome*. The answer is this: establish the target slightly in front of the opponent's vital point. It can then be hit in a controlled way with maximum power, without making contact.

Training transforms various parts of the body into weapons to be used freely and effectively. The quality necessary to accomplish this is self-control. To become a victor, one must first overcome his own self.

KATA

The *kata* of karate-dō are logical arrangements of blocking, punching, striking and kicking techniques in certain set sequences. About fifty kata, or "formal exercises," are practiced at the present time, some having been passed down from generation to generation, others having been developed fairly recently.

Kata can be divided into two broad categories. In one group are those appropriate for physical development, the strengthening of bone and muscle. Though seemingly simple, they require composure for their performance and exhibit strength and dignity when correctly performed. In the other group are kata suitable for the development of fast reflexes and the ability to move quickly. The lightninglike movements in these kata are suggestive of the rapid flight of the swallow. All kata require and foster rhythm and coordination.

Training in kata is spiritual as well as physical. In his performance of the kata, the karateka should exhibit boldness and confidence, but also humility, gentleness and a sense of decorum, thus integrating mind and body in a singular discipline. As Gichin Funakoshi often reminded his students, "The spirit of karate-dō is lost without courtesy."

One expression of this courtesy is the bow made at the beginning and at the end of each kata. The stance is the *musubi-dachi* (informal attention stance), with the arms relaxed, the hands lightly touching the thighs and the eyes focused straight ahead.

From the bow at the start of the kata, one moves into the *kamae* of the first movement of the kata. This is a relaxed position, so tenseness, particularly in the shoulders and knees, should be eliminated and breathing should be relaxed. The center of power and concentration is the *tanden*, the center of gravity. In this position, the karateka should be prepared for any eventuality and full of fighting spirit.

Being relaxed but alert also characterizes the bow at the end of the kata and is called *zanshin*. In karate-dō, as in other martial arts, bringing the kata to a perfect finish is of the greatest importance.

Each kata begins with a blocking technique and consists of a specific number of movements to be performed in a particular order. There is some variation in the complexity of the movements and the time required to complete them, but each movement has its own meaning and function and nothing is superfluous. Performance is along the *embusen* (performance line), the shape of which is decided for each kata.

While performing a kata, the karateka should imagine himself to be surrounded by opponents and be prepared to execute defensive and offensive techniques in any direction.

Mastery of kata is a prerequsite for advancement through *kyū* and *dan* as follows:

8th *kyū*	Heian 1
7th *kyū*	Heian 2
6th *kyū*	Heian 3
5th *kyū*	Heian 4
4th *kyū*	Heian 5
3rd *kyū*	Tekki 1
2nd *kyū*	Kata other than Heian or Tekki
1st *kyū*	Other than the above
1st *dan*	Other than the above
2nd *dan* and above	Free kata

Free kata may be chosen from Bassai, Kankū, Jitte, Hangetsu, Empi, Gankaku, Jion, Tekki, Nijūshihō, Gojūshihō, Unsu, Sōchin, Meikyō, Chinte, Wankan and others.

Important Points

Since the effects of practice are cumulative, practice every day, even if only for a few minutes. When performing a kata, keep calm and never rush through the movements. This means always being aware of the correct timing of each movement. If a particular kata proves difficult, give it more attention, and always keep in mind the relationship between kata practice and kumite (see Vols. 3 and 4).

Specific points in performance are:

1. *Correct order.* The number and sequence of movements is predetermined. All must be performed.

2. *Beginning and end.* The kata must begin and end at the same spot on the *embusen.* This requires practice.

3. *Meaning of each movement.* Each movement, defensive or offensive must be clearly understood and fully expressed. This is also true of the kata as a whole, each of which has its own characteristics.

4. *Awareness of the target.* The karateka must know what the target is and when to execute a technique.

5. *Rhythm and timing.* Rhythm must be appropriate to the particular kata and the body must be flexible, never overstrained. Remember the three factors of the correct use of power, swiftness or slowness in executing techniques, and the stretching and contraction of muscles.

6. *Proper breathing.* Breathing should change with changing situations, but basically inhale when blocking, exhale

when a finishing technique is executed, and inhale and exhale when executing successive techniques.

Related to breathing is the *kiai*, which occurs in the middle or at the end of the kata, at the moment of maximum tension. By exhaling very sharply and tensing the abdomen, extra power can be given to the muscles.

Rhythm

JITTE

1 2 3·4 5 6·7 8·9·10 11 12·13 14▲15 16 17a 17b
18a·18b 19 20 21 22·23 24▲

HANGETSU

1·2 3·4 5·6 7 8 9 10▲11 12 13 14 15 16 17·18·19
20·21·22 23·24·25 26 27 28·29·30·31 32 33 34·35·36·37 38
39 40 41▲

EMPI

1 2 3 4 5 6·7·8 9 10·11·12 13 14 15 16 17 18 19 20
21 22 23 24 25 26 27 28 29 30 31 32 33 34 35·36 37▲

╌╌╌	continuous, fast	—	powerfully
⌒	strong, continuous, fast	‿	slow, powerfully
‿	strong	▲ ▲	pause
◄	increasingly strong	✧	*kiai*

1
JITTE

Yōi

Flex elbows, lightly cover right fist with left hand and bring hands in front of chin (20 cm.) for *kamae*.

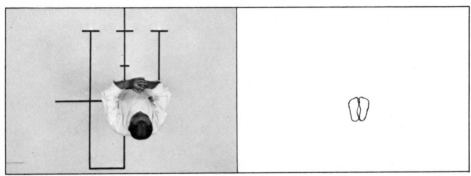

Heisoku-dachi

1 Uhai tekubi chūdan osae-uke
Hidari ken hidari koshi

Middle level pressing block with back of right wrist / *Left fist at left side.* Bend right wrist fully, fingers at middle joints.

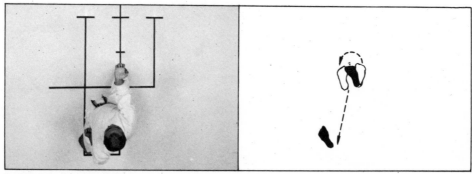

1. Migi zenkutsu-dachi

2 Migi teishō gedan osae-uke
Hidari teishō chūdan oshi-age-uke

Lower level pressing block with right palm-heel / Middle level pressing-rising block with left palm-heel. Do 1 and 2 slowly.

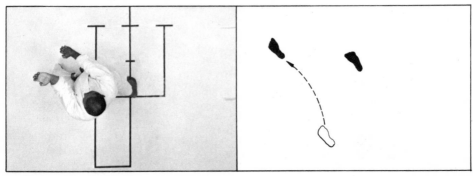

2. Hidari zenkutsu-dachi

3   *Hidari shō chūdan osae-uke*

Middle level pressing block with left hand   Turn head to right, bring left forearm parallel to chest. Keep elbow in place.

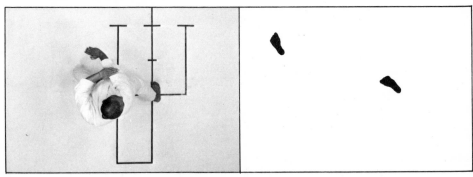

3.

4

Migi shō tekubi migi sokumen chūdan kake-uke
Hidari ken hidari koshi

Middle level hooking block to right side with right hand-wrist |
Left fist at left side *Yori-ashi*, half step to right.

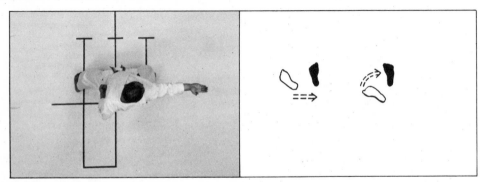

4. Kiba-dachi

5

Migi teishō migi sokumen chūdan yoko uchi
Hidari ken hidari koshi

Middle level side strike to right with right palm-heel | Left fist at left side Left leg is pivot. Bend right elbow slightly.

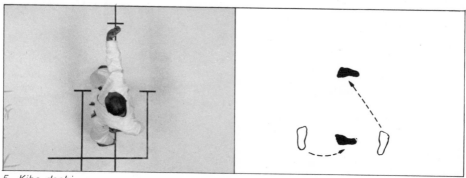

5. Kiba-dachi

6

Hidari teishō hidari sokumen chūdan yoko uchi
Migi ken migi koshi

Middle level side strike to left with left palm-heel | Right fist at right side With right leg as pivot, rotate hips to right.

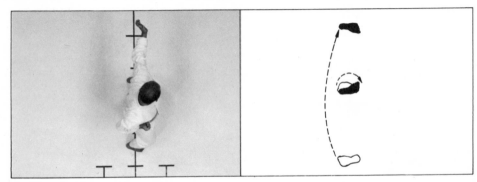

6. Kiba-dachi

7

Migi teishō migi sokumen chūdan yoko uchi
Hidari ken hidari koshi

Middle level side strike to right with right palm-heel | Left fist at left side With left leg as pivot, rotate hips to left.

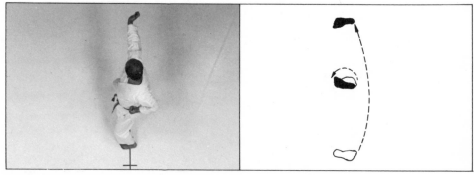

7. *Kiba-dachi*

Ryō ken jōdan jūji uke

Upper level X block with both fists Right wrist in front for X
block.

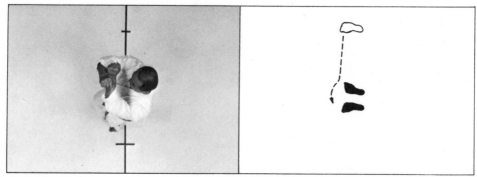

8. Migi ashi mae kōsa-dachi

9   *Ryō ken ryō soku gedan uchi-barai*

Lower level sweeping block to both sides with both fists Backs
of both fists outward ; hands no more than 20 cm. from body.

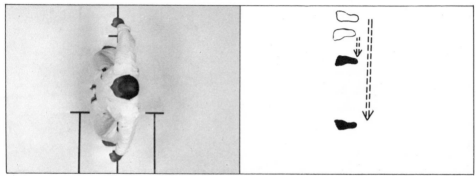

9. *Kiba-dachi*

10 *Yama-gamae (Jōdan kakiwake uke)*

Mountain posture (Upper level reverse wedge block) Gradual *yori-ashi* to left. Cross arms in front of chest.

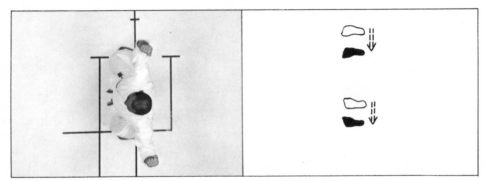

10. *Kiba-dachi*

Upper level side-sweeping block with left wrist Keeping mountain posture, turn head to right, rotate hips to right.

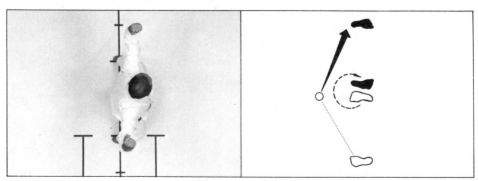

11. *Kiba-dachi*

12 *Migi ken tekubi jōdan yoko uchi-barai*

Upper level side-sweeping block with right wrist Rotate hips to left.

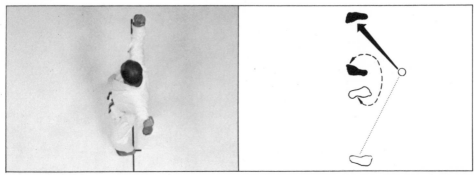

12. *Kiba-dachi*

13 *Hidari ken tekubi jōdan yoko uchi-barai*

Upper level side-sweeping block with left wrist Rotate hips to right. Turn head in harmony with hip rotation.

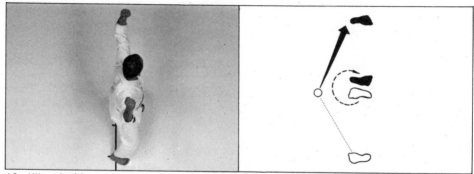

13. *Kiba-dachi*

14 *Ryō ken tai soku ni kakiwake orosu*

Thrusting both fists down to sides of body Both feet in place,
lightly straighten knees. Calmly withdraw power.

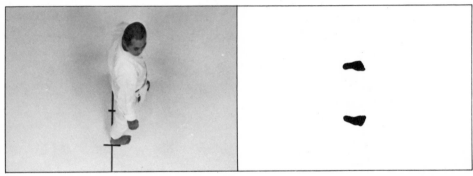

14.

15

Migi shutō jōdan uke
Hidari ken hidari koshi

Upper level block with right sword hand / Left fist at left side
Turn face to right, quickly bring right hand diagonally upward.

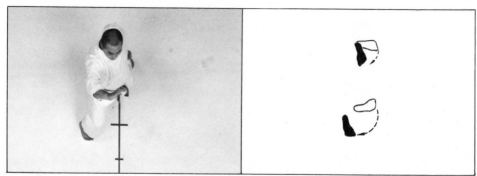

15. *Migi zenkutsu-dachi*

16 Ryō shō kokō bō uke

Blocking stick attack with tiger mouths Turn torso slightly to right. Hands should form a straight vertical line.

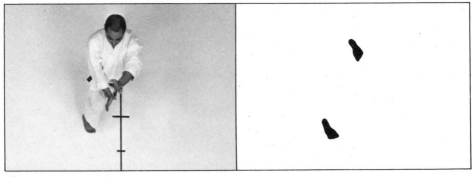

16.

17 a
Migi shō migi kata ue
Hidari shō migi waki

Right hand above right shoulder / *Left hand at right side of chest* Rotate hips to right. Raise left leg high.

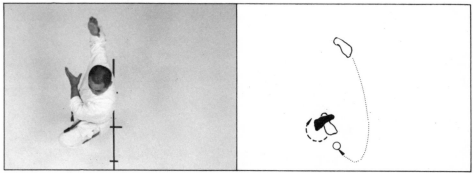

17a. Migi ashi-dachi

Migi shō jōdan oshidashi
Hidari shō gedan oshidashi

Upper level thrust with right hand | Lower level thrust with left hand Quickly advance left foot, gradually apply power.

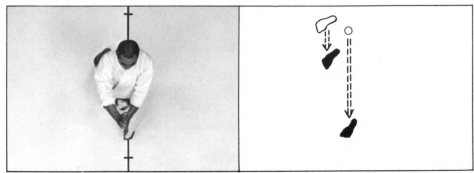

17b. Hidari zenkutsu-dachi

Hidari shō hidari kata ue
Migi shō hidari waki

Left hand above left shoulder / Right hand at left side of body
Turn torso slightly to left.

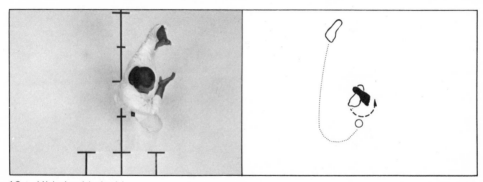

1.8a. Hidari ashi-dachi

18 b   *Hidari shō jōdan oshidashi*
Migi shō gedan oshidashi

*Upper level thrust with left hand / Lower level thrust with right
hand   Yori-ashi* with right foot (rather like stamping kick).

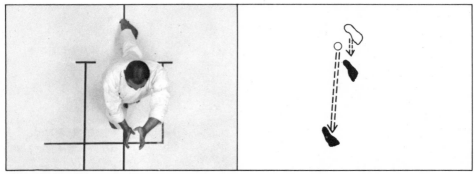

18b. Migi zenkutsu-dachi

19

Migi ken migi sokumen jōdan uchi uke
Hidari ken hidari sokumen gedan uke

Upper level block, inside outward, to right side with right fist / Lower level block to left side with left fist

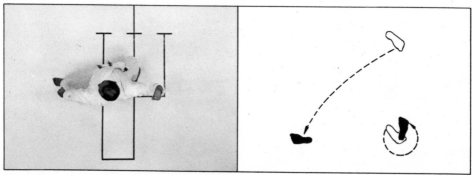

19. Migi kōkutsu-dachi

20

Hidari ken hidari sokumen jōdan uchi uke
Migi ken migi sokumen gedan uke

Upper level block, inside outward, to left side with left fist /
Lower level block to right side with right fist

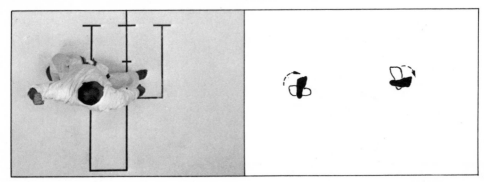

20. *Hidari kōkutsu-dachi*

21 *Hidari ken jōdan age-uke*

Upper level rising block with left fist

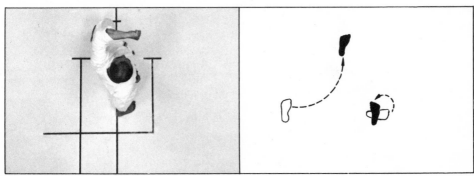

21. *Hidari zenkutsu-dachi*

22 Migi jōdan age-uke

Right upper level rising block

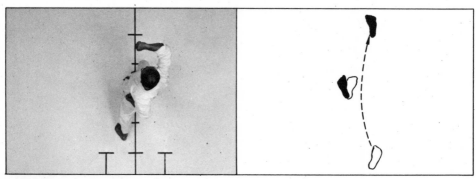

22. Migi zenkutsu-dachi

Hidari jōdan age-uke

Left upper level rising block to left. With right leg as pivot, rotate hips

23. *Hidari zenkutsu-dachi*

24 Migi jōdan age-uke

YA!

Right upper level rising block

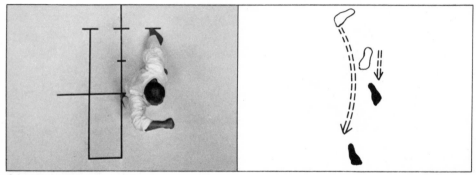

24. Migi zenkutsu-dachi

Naore

Right leg is pivot. While turning to left, draw left foot to right foot, return to posture of *yōi*.

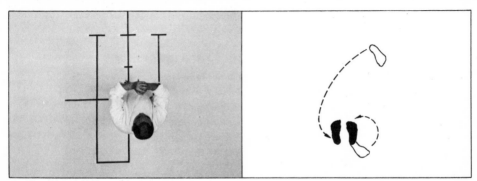

Shizen-tai

JITTE: IMPORTANT POINTS

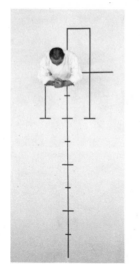

The idea implicit in the name *Jitte* is that mastery of this kata should enable one to perform the actions of ten men. From it can be learned techniques for dealing with weapon attacks, particularly stick attacks.

To block strongly, various important points found also in the Heian 3 kata, such as the crucial role of the hips in concentrating power, must be completely mastered. This kata is effective for tempering bone and sinew and for understanding the importance of and mastering the tightening of the sides of the chest, for example in twisting the torso after blocking, overturning the opponent or taking the opponent by force.

Twenty-four movements. About one minute.

1. Movement 1 : Against a stick attack coming diagonally from the front, swing the forearm down from chin level.
Movement 2 : Turn the right wrist over, grasping the stick, and push upward with the left hand. The timing of pushing—downward and upward—is very important. Bend wrists fully into right angles. Opponent's strike can be blocked with downward push of right palm-heel. Strike his jaw with left palm-heel.

2. Movements 5–6: Against a stick attack from the front, rotate right hip to take straddle-leg stance. Sweep stick to one side with right palm-heel, grasp it and bring left foot forward. Grasp stick with left hand, with the feeling of sweeping from the opposite direction. Coordination of hand movement and hip rotation, split-second timing and sufficient tightening of the sides of the chest are necessary.

3

4

5

3.   Movement 8–9 : Against a stick attack from the front, take
crossed-feet stance, cross hands, thrust upward, blocking with
upper level X block. Sliding left foot to the left, grasp stick with
right hand, dispose of it to right side.

4.   Movement 10 : Against an attack aimed at the face, cross
hands in front of face and block with upper side of right forearm.
Slide feet to the left.

5.   Movement 12 : Against a stick attack to the face, sweep
aside with little-finger side of the wrist in a movement coordinated with hip rotation. At the same time, raise knee high and
stamp-kick opponent's thigh or the back of his foot. When
rotating hips and blocking, abdomen, chest and both arms
should have the solidness of a single board.

6. Movements 15–17: If the opponent brings the stick down from above his head, block with right sword hand. Turning the wrist over, grasp the stick and with the elbow as the center of the movement, push downward. Push upward with the left hand at the same time. If opponent persists, raise right hand high to the side of the head and capture the stick with the feeling of swinging it around. When either blocking or capturing the stick, do not swing the arms widely. Tighten the sides of the chest firmly. Keep stick close to the opponent's body.

$\frac{2}{\text{HANGETSU}}$

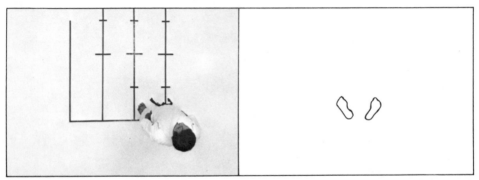

Hachinoji-dachi shizen-tai

1. Hidari chūdan uchi uke

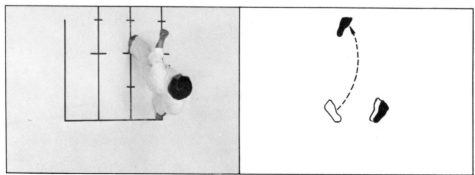

Left middle level block, inside outward Slide left foot in semicircle. Swing left fist slowly, gradually applying power.

1. Hidari mae hangetsu-dachi

Migi chūdan choku-zuki

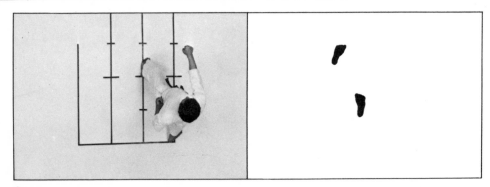

Right middle level straight punch

2.

3   *Migi chūdan uchi uke*

Right middle level block, inside outward

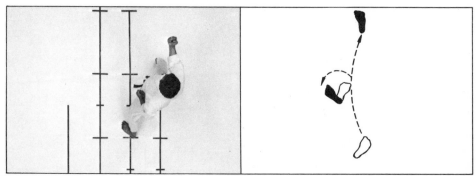

3. Migi mae hangetsu-dachi

4 Hidari chūdan choku-zuki

Left middle level straight punch

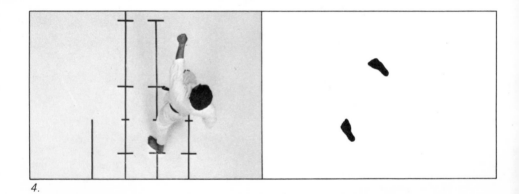

4.

Hidari chūdan uchi uke

Left middle level block, inside outward

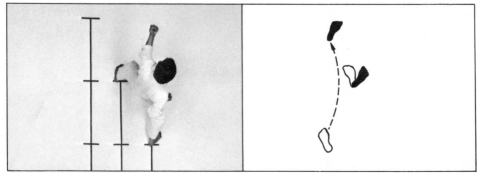

5. *Hidari mae hangetsu-dachi*

6 *Migi chūdan choku-zuki*

Right middle level straight punch

6.

One-knuckle fists in front of nipples kamae Thrust left fist forward, align fists and bring back to nipples together.

7.

8 *Ryō ippon ken chūdan choku-zuki*

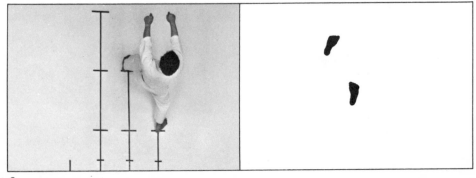

Middle level straight punches with one-knuckle fists

8.

9 *Ryō shō yama-gamae*

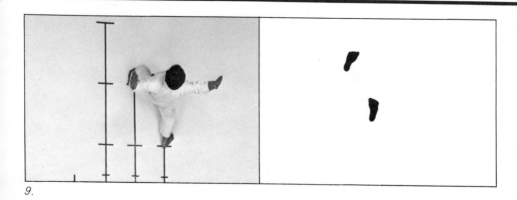

Both hands mountain posture   Form right angles with elbows.
Arms and head resemble character for mountain (山).

9.

Ryō shō ryō soku gedan barai

Downward block to sides with both hands Do Movements 1–10 slowly, quietly. At *kime*, apply power fully.

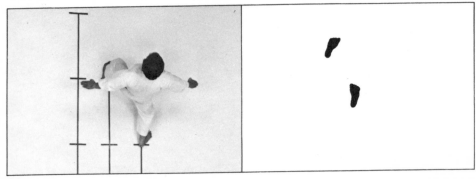

10.

11 Migi shō chūdan uchi uke
Hidari shō gedan barai

Middle level block, inside outward, with right hand | Downward block with left hand Extend index fingers, lightly bend others.

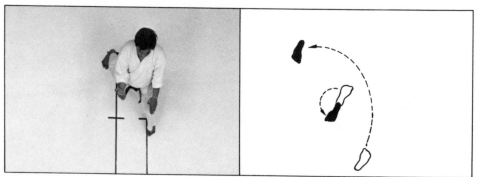

11. Hidari mae hangetsu-dachi

12 Migi shō tsukami-uke
Hidari shō sono mama

Grasping block with right hand/Left hand as is Bringing right elbow slightly toward right side, turn right wrist over.

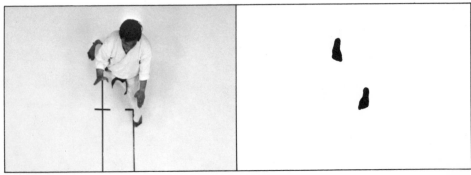

12.

13

Hidari shō chūdan uchi uke
Migi shō gedan barai

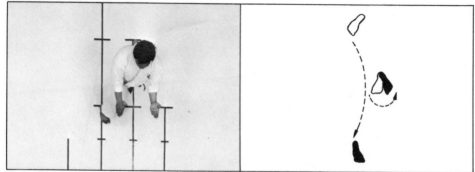

*Middle level block, inside outward, with left hand / Downward
block with right hand*

13. Migi mae hangetsu-dachi

14 *Hidari shō tsukami-uke*

Grasping block with left hand Perform this movement slowly.

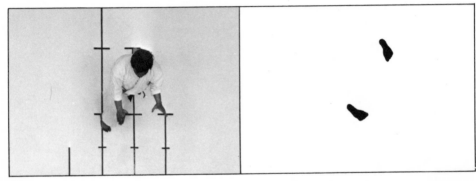

14.

15

Migi shō chūdan uchi uke
Hidari shō gedan barai

Middle level block, inside outward, with right hand / Downward
block with left hand

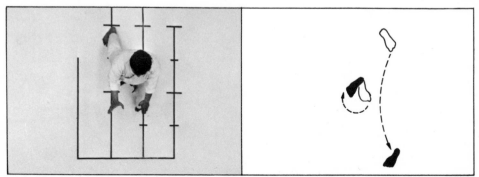

15. Hidari mae hangetsu-dachi

16 *Migi shō tsukami-uke*

Grasping block with right hand   Perform slowly.

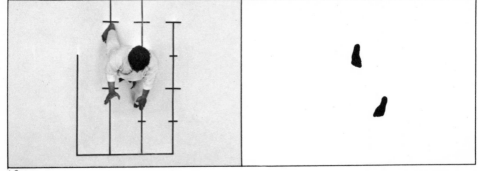

16.

17

Migi ken chūdan uchi uke
Hidari ken hidari koshi

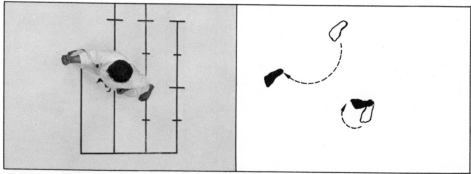

Middle level block, inside outward, with right fist | Left fist at left side Slide right foot in half-moon arc to the side.

17. *Migi mae hangetsu-dachi*

Middle level straight punch with left fist

Middle level straight punch with right fist

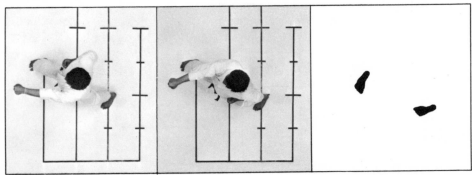

18.

19.

20. Hidari ken chūdan uchi uke

Middle level block, inside outward, with left fist   *Yori-ashi,* to face in opposite direction.

20. *Hidari mae hangetsu-dachi*

21 *Migi ken chūdan choku-zuki*   ## 22 *Hidari ken chūdan choku-zuki*

Middle level straight punch with right fist

Middle level straight punch with left fist

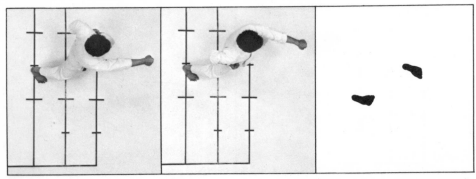

21.   22.

23 *Migi ken chūdan uchi uke*

Middle level block, inside outward, with right fist Slight
yori-ashi.

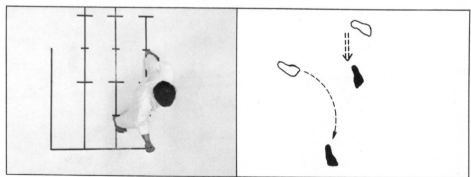

23. *Migi mae hangetsu-dachi*

24 Hidari ken chūdan choku-zuki

25 Migi ken chūdan choku-zuki

Middle level straight punch with left fist

Middle level straight punch with right fist

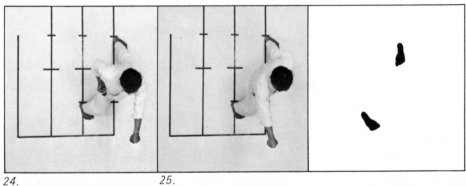

24.   25.

Hidari uraken tate mawashi-uchi
Migi ken migi koshi

Vertical strike with left back-fist / Right fist at right side   While rotating hips to left, bring left sole to right knee and raise leg.

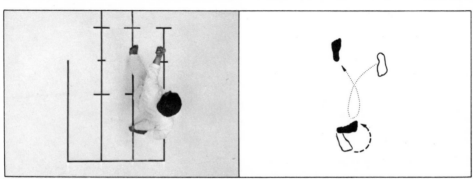

26. Migi kōkutsu-dachi

Hidari ken sono mama
Migi ken migi koshi

Left fist as is / Right fist at right side   Slowly, quietly.

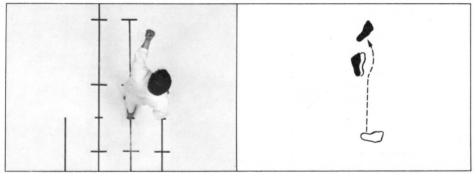

27. *Hidari ashi-dachi*

28 *Hidari ken migi kata ue e hiku*
Hidari mae keage

Bring left fist above right shoulder / Left front snap kick Shift body weight to right leg. Raise hand and kick simultaneously.

28. Migi ashi-dachi

Hidari ken gedan-zuki

Lower level punch with left fist Lower kicking leg in front of right leg. Strike rather low.

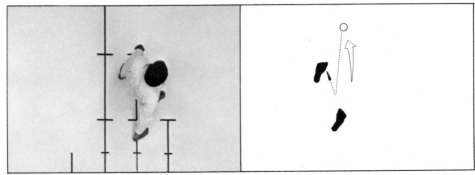

29. *Hidari mae hangetsu-dachi*

30 Migi ken chūdan-zuki

Middle level punch with right fist   Twist hips to left.

30.

31 *Hidari jōdan age-uke*

Left upper level rising block

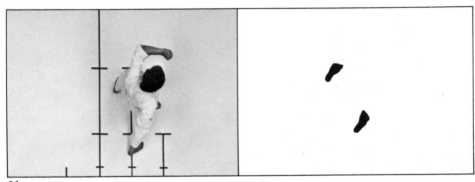

31.

Vertical strike with right back-fist Rotate hips to right, reverse direction.

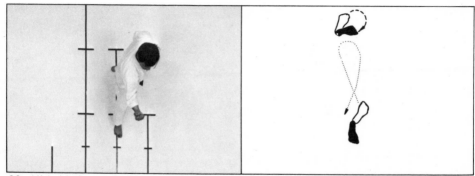

32. Hidari kōkutsu-dachi

33 Sono mama

Posture as is

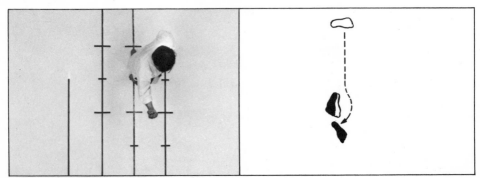

33. Migi ashi-dachi

34 *Migi ken hidari kata ue e hiku*
Migi mae keage

Bring right fist above left shoulder / *Right front snap kick*

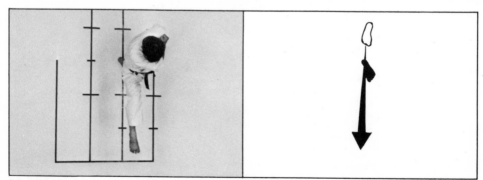

34. *Hidari ashi-dachi*

35 *Migi ken gedan-zuki*

Lower level punch with right fist

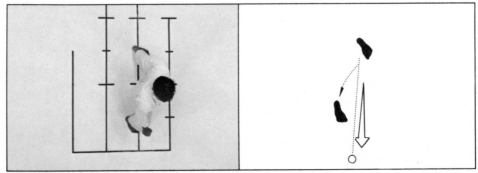

35. Migi mae hangetsu-dachi

36 | *Ḥidari ken chūdan-zuki*   ## 37 | *Migi jōdan age-uke*

Middle level punch with left fist

Right upper level rising block

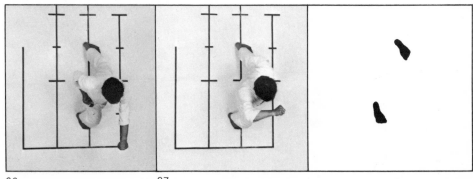

36.   37.

38 *Hidari uraken tate mawashi-uchi*

Vertical strike with left back-fist Rotate hips to left, reverse direction. Swing left fist from right hip above head.

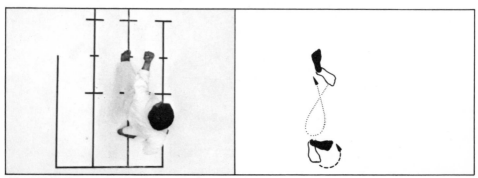

38. *Migi kōkutsu-dachi*

39 *Migi chūdan mikazuki-geri*

Right middle level crescent kick
Kick left palm with right foot.

Shift body weight to left leg.

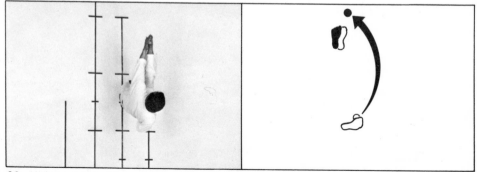

39. *Hidari ashi-dachi*

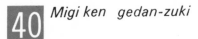

40 Migi ken gedan-zuki

Lower level punch with right fist Bring kicking leg down to the rear.

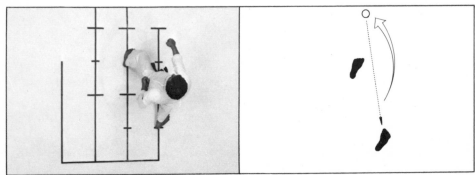

40. *Hidari mae hangetsu-dachi*

Gedan gasshō uke

Lower level block with palm-heels together Slowly bring hands to sides, then thrust palm-heels forward together.

41. *Hidari mae neko-ashi-dachi*

Naore

Withdrawing left leg, return to position of *yōi*.

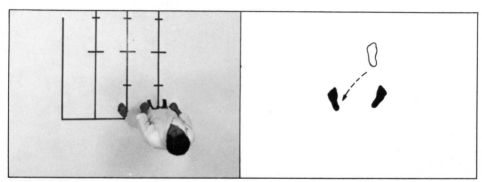

Shizen-tai

HANGETSU: IMPORTANT POINTS

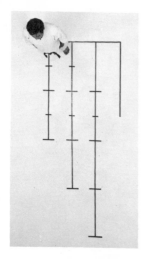

As this kata, once called Seishan, developed, it came to be known as Hangetsu (half-moon) from the semicircular movements of the hands and feet.

Fast and slow techniques, hand and foot movements coordinated with breathing and sliding the feet in arc-shaped movements are characteristic of this kata. The foot movements are always useful for getting inside the opponent's legs, attacking and destroying his balance. The foot-sliding movements in Hangetsu are most effective for close-in attacks.

Forty-one movements. About one minute.

1

2

1. Hangetsu-dachi: Slightly narrower than the front stance, both feet are turned in toward the line connecting the insteps and both knees are twisted inward. It is important that both heels and outside edges of the feet (*sokutō*) be firmly planted.
2. Movement 7: While making one-kunckle fist, bring right hand toward right nipple. Begin movement of left hand at the same time. When it is aligned with right hand, turn wrist over and in unison with right hand bring it back to left nipple.

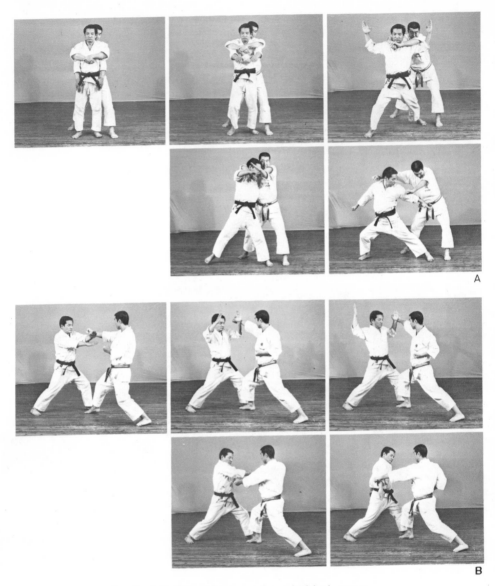

A

B

3. Movements 9–10: (A) When hugged from behind, opponent's arms can be loosened by stepping strongly forward, bending elbows and raising arms. This will not be effective unless arms are raised and foot is slid forward at the same time. (B) Sweep aside an upper level attack from the inside outward by using the upper side of the forearm (*haiwan*). If opponent attacks to middle level, sweep-block with *haiwan*, swinging hand downward and outward from above your head.

4. Movements 11–12: After blocking with sword hand, turn wrist over, grab opponent's arm and pull. Counterattack with other sword hand. Do not pull captured arm farther than the side of your own body. Closing the armpit is very important.

5. Movement 26: When your back leg is the target of a kick, raise your knee to chest level. At the time the foot is lowered, attack opponent's face with vertical back-fist. Bend and lock the ankle and knee of the supporting leg to maintain balance.

6.   Movements 27–29 : When wrist is grasped and distance is not right for either kicking or fist attack, do not move captured arm. Calmly, so opponent does not understand the movement, cross back foot in front of front foot. Immediately counterattack with middle level kick, bringing freed hand above the shoulder. In kumite, when distance is too great for either kicking or punching, without moving fist or torso, quietly and quickly cross back foot in front of front foot. Then kick.

7

8

7. Movements 39–40: Blocking a middle level attack with a crescent kick, withdraw the kicking leg and at the same time counterattack with middle level punch. The important point of the crescent kick is raising the knee high.

8. Movement 41: Against a kicking attack, bring back front leg for cat leg stance, block using both palm-heels together. If hips are unstable, it is difficult to respond to a strong kick, so it is much more effective, instead of withdrawing leg, to do this by positioning hips over back supporting heel.

$$\frac{3}{EMPI}$$

Yōi

Left hand at left side (palm to the right). Right fist at left palm
(back of hand to the front).

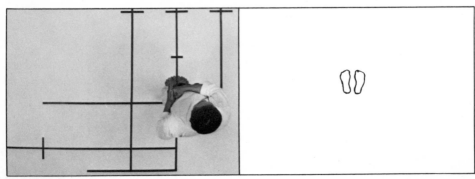

Shizen-tai

1 *Migi ken gedan barai*
Hidari ken migi mune mae kamae

Downward block with right fist / Left fist in front of right side of chest kamae Right knee lightly touching left heel.

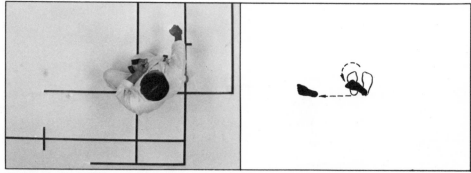

1. Migi ashi orishiku

Both fists at left side kamae Back of left fist downward. Back of
right fist to the front.

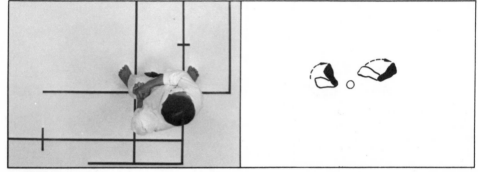

2. Hachinoji-dachi

Migi gedan barai

Right downward block

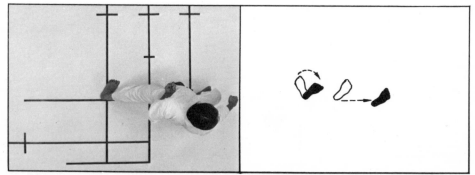

3. Migi hiza kussu

4

*Hidari ude mizu-nagare kamae
Migi ken migi koshi*

Left arm flowing water position | Right fist at right side Turn
head to front.

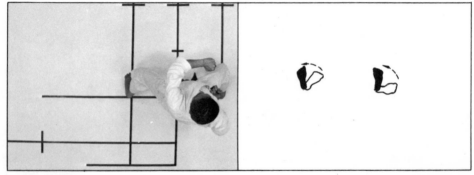

4. Kiba-dachi

Left downward block

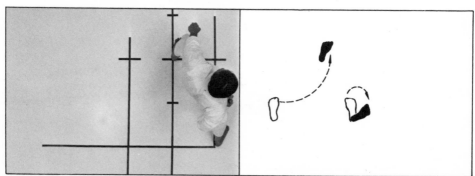

5. *Hidari zenkutsu-dachi*

6 Migi ken jōdan age-zuki

Upper level rising punch with right fist Turn torso slightly to left.

6.

7

Migi ken hidari kata ue
Hidari ken gedan-zuki

Right fist above left shoulder / Downward punch with left fist
Open right hand, then make fist. Pull it back strongly.

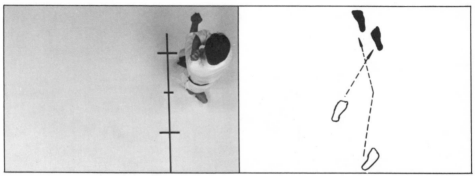

7. *Migi ashi-dachi*

Right downward block / Left fist at left side Bring left foot
one step back. Right wrist passes close above left arm.

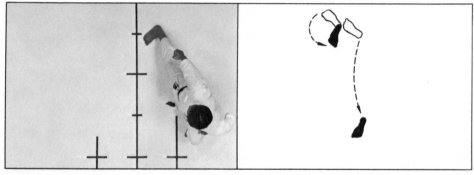

8. *Hidari hiza kussu* 運足 7

9 *Hidari gedan barai*

Left downward block   Rotate hips to left, reverse direction.

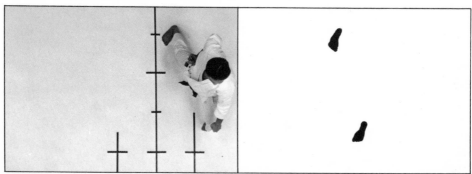

9. *Hidari zenkutsu-dachi*

Migi ken jōdan age-zuki

Upper level rising punch with right fist Turn torso slightly to
left.

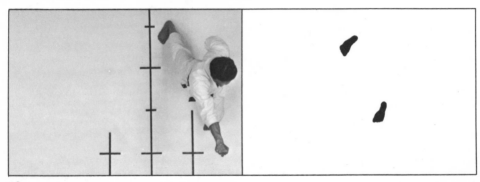

10.

11

Migi ken hidari kata ue
Hidari ken gedan-zuki

Right fist above left shoulder / Downward punch with left fist
Jump one step forward. Cross left foot behind right heel.

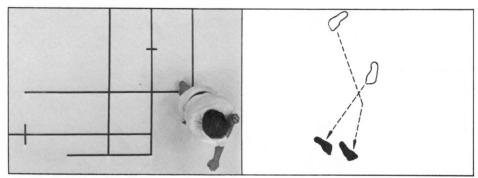

11. *Migi ashi-dachi*

Migi gedan barai

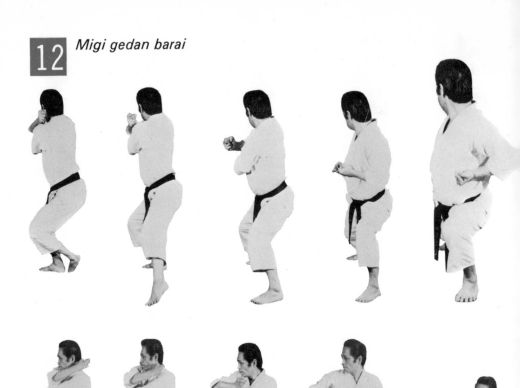

Right downward block Incline torso slightly to left.

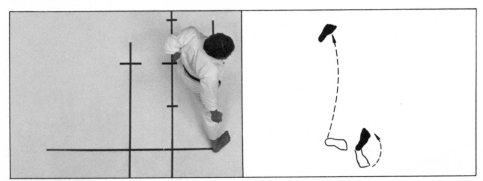

12. *Hidari hiza kussu*

13 *Hidari gedan barai*

Left downward block Feet in place, reverse direction of upper body.

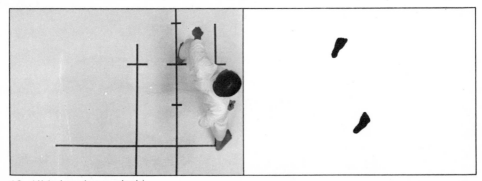

13. *Hidari zenkutsu-dachi*

14 Hidari shō hidari naname zempō kamae
Migi ken migi koshi

Left hand diagonally to left front kamae / Right fist at right side
Raise torso, shift weight to right leg. Do slowly.

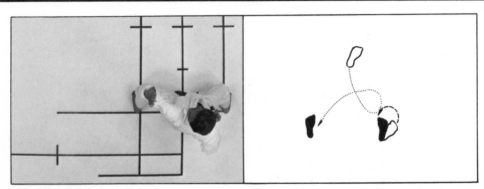

14. Kiba-dachi

15 *Migi ken tekubi hidari shō uchiate*

Strike left hand with right wrist Swing right fist widely, back of fist to the front. Turn head to the front.

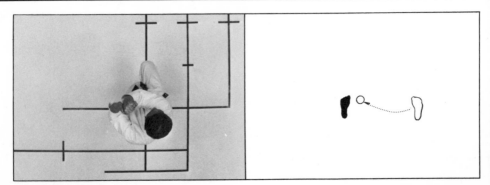

15. *Hidari ashi-dachi*

16 *Hidari tate shutō chūdan uke*
Migi ken migi koshi

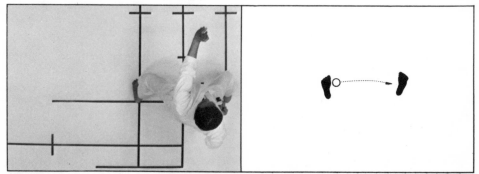

16. *Kiba-dachi*

*Middle level block with left vertical sword hand / Right fist at
right side* Swing left hand from right armpit. Open right hand.

17 *Migi ken chūdan-zuki*

Middle level straight punch with right fist

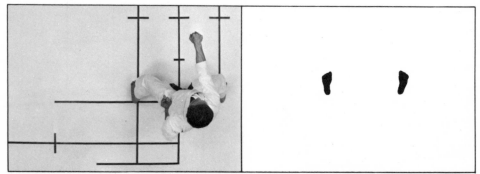

17.

18 *Hidari ken chūdan choku-zuki*

19 *Hidari gedan barai*

Middle level straight punch with left fist   Left downward block

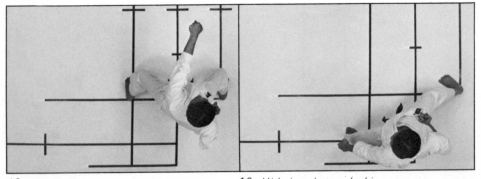

18.   19. *Hidari zenkutsu-dachi*

20 *Migi jōdan age-zuki*

Right upper level rising punch   Turn torso slightly to left.

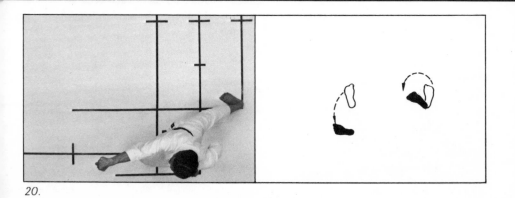

20.

Migi shutō chūdan-uke

Middle level block with right sword hand

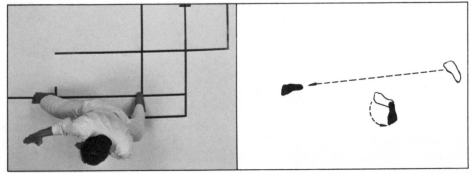

21. *Hidari kōkutsu-dachi*

22 Hidari shutō chūdan-uke

*Middle level block with left sword hand   Reverse position of
feet. In Movements 21–22, turn hips fast.

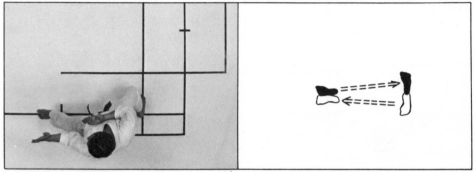

22. Migi kōkutsu-dachi

Middle level punch with right fist

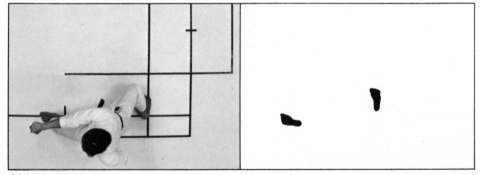

23.

Migi shutō chūdan uke

Middle level block with right sword hand

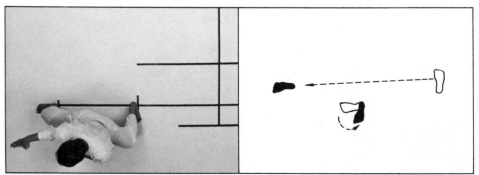

24. Hidari kōkutsu-dachi

25 *Hidari gedan barai*

Left downward block With right leg as pivot, rotate hips to left, reverse direction.

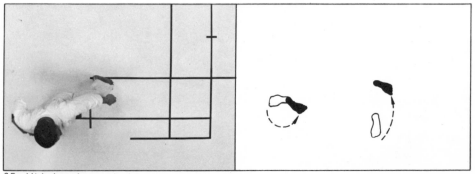

25. *Hidari zenkutsu-dachi*

Migi ken jōdan age-zuki

Upper level rising punch with right fist Turn torso slightly to left.

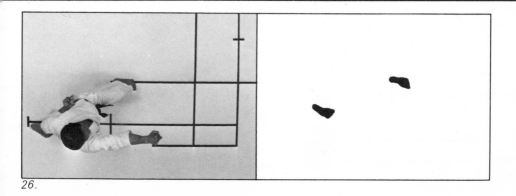

26.

27 *Migi ken hidari kata ue*
Hidari ken gedan-zuki

Right fist above left shoulder / Downward punch with left fist
Jump one step forward. Cross left foot behind right heel.

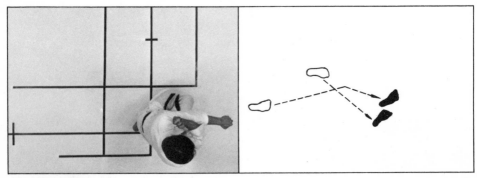

27. *Migi ashi-dachi*

28 *Migi gedan barai*
Hidari ken hidari koshi

Right downward block | Left fist at left side Bring left foot one
step back. Incline torso slightly to left.

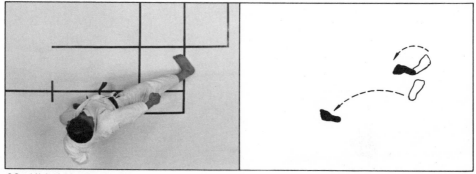

28. *Hidari hiza kussu*

Hidari gedan barai
Migi ken migi koshi

Left downward block / Right fist at right side With feet in place, turn upper body in opposite direction.

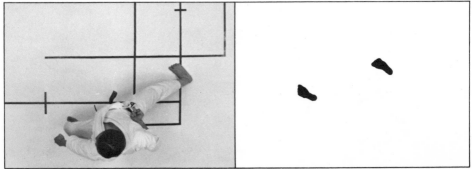

29. Hidari zenkutsu-dachi

126

Migi teishō chūdan oshi-age-uke
Hidari ken hidari koshi

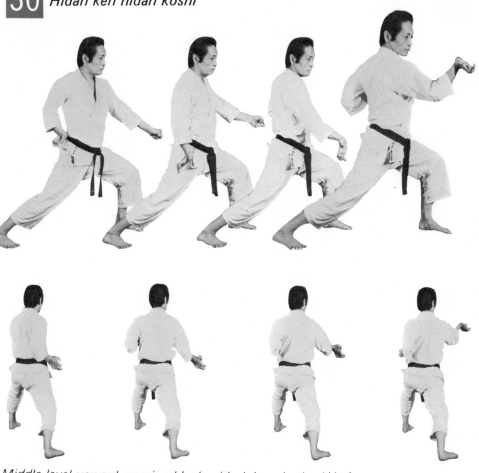

Middle level upward pressing block with right palm-heel / Left fist at left side Gradually apply power. Bend wrist fully.

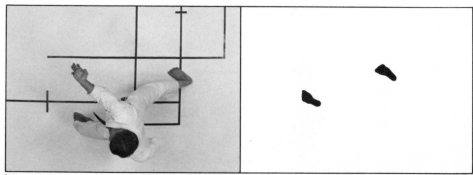

30.

31 *Migi teishō chūdan oshi-age-uke*
Hidari teishō gedan osae-uke

*Middle level upward pressing block with right palm-heel / Lower
level pressing block with left palm-heel* Bend left wrist fully.

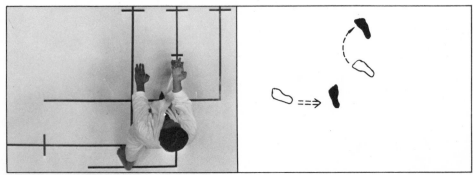

31. *Migi zenkutsu-dachi*

Hidari teishō chūdan oshi-age-uke
Migi teishō gedan osae-uke

Middle level upward pressing block with left palm-heel / Lower
level pressing block with right palm-heel

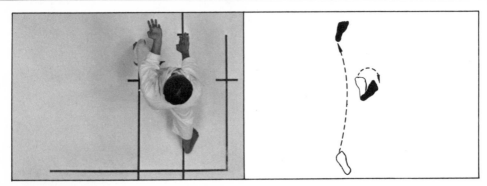

32. *Hidari zenkutsu-dachi*

33 *Migi teishō chūdan oshi-age-uke*
Hidari teishō gedan osae-uke

Middle level upward pressing block with right palm-heel / Lower
level pressing block with left palm-heel

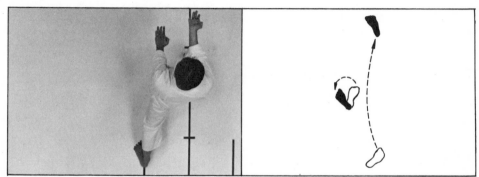

33. *Migi zenkutsu-dachi*

Migi ken gedan-gamae
Hidari ken hidari koshi

Right fist lower level kamae | Left fist at left side Twisting right
hand, bring it downward from left shoulder.

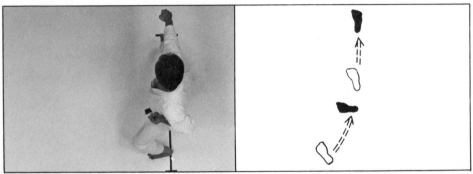

34. Hidari kōkutsu-dachi

35 Migi shō gedan ni oshidasu
Hidari shō jōdan tsukami-uke

*Lower level thrust with right hand / Upper level grasping block
with left hand* Incline torso slightly forward.

35. *Migi mae hiza kussu*

36 *Migi shutō chūdan uke*

Middle level block with right sword hand Jump high, turning to left. Land in back stance. Move hands above head.

36. Hidari kōkutsu-dachi

37 Hidari shutō chūdan uke

Middle level block with left sword hand

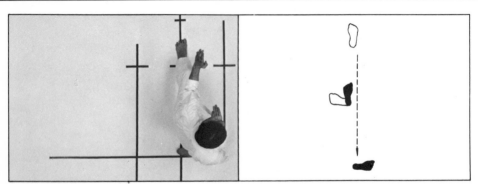

37. Migi kōkutsu-dachi

Naore

Withdraw left foot to return to position of *yōi*.

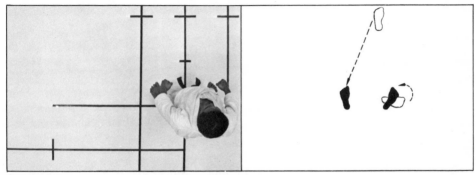

Shizen-tai

EMPI: IMPORTANT POINTS

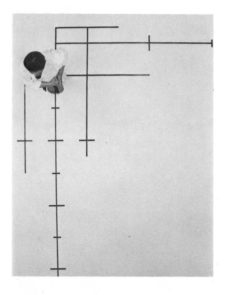

This is the kata formerly known as Wanshū.

The meaning of the name *Empi*, "flying swallow," is found in the upper level rising strike and in jumping and striking while grasping the opponent and pulling him in, which are suggestive of the high and low flight of the swallow. And in reversing direction, which is like flying. This is a light and easy kata, keen and quick-witted.

Encountering the opponent, when one's hand is obstructed, one can discover techniques and openings, invite the opponent's attack and learn from the exchange of tactics.

Thirty-seven movements. About one minute.

A

B

1. Movement 1: (A) Blocking a punch from the right side with the left hand, pull the opponent down, slide left foot to the left and catch his knee with the right wrist.
(B) In sweep blocking a kick from the front with the right forearm, the important point is the sharp rotation of the hips to the left. Open left leg, kneel and block simultaneously.

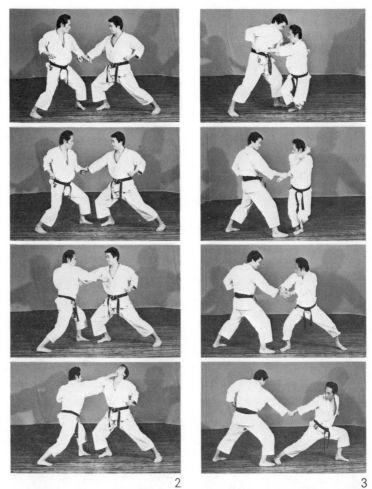

2   3

2. Movement 7: Striking the opponent's jaw with a right rising strike, open fist and grasp him by hair or chest. While pulling him in, jump and strike to the middle level. The crossed-feet stance is done correctly by bringing the left foot behind the right heel. The important points in jumping are bending the knees, lowering the hips and supporting all the body weight on the right leg. No matter how deeply the hips are bent, do not lean in back of the right heel.

3. Movement 8: If in Movement 7 the opponent grasps the striking left hand, strike his arm to free it. This can be done by hitting a vital point in the opponent's arm. The important point in going from the crossed-feet stance to the back stance is rotating the hips rapidly. Execute downward block by twisting the right wrist from above the left forearm.

4. Movements 14–16: While raising left hand to eye level, shift left leg to the left for straddle-leg stance. Raise left knee high, hold left elbow and knee in space at the same time, then swing widely and slowly. Concentrate eyes on the left hand. When neither you nor the opponent can move and you are obstructed by his hand, move the left hand slowly and widely to take him by surprise. Thrust the right hand up, strike his left hand, deliberately making an opening and inviting an attack. Counterattack by striking the attacking hand. Or, without inviting an attack, while sweeping away opponent's upper level strike, attack his face strongly with the right hand.

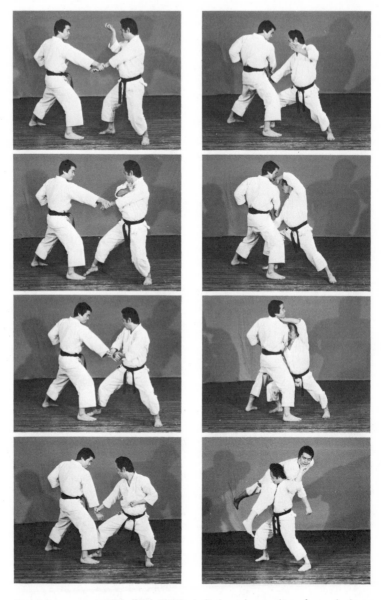

5. Movements 34–35: With left hand coming from below and right hand from left shoulder, hands move up and down together in a wringing motion. Advancing by *yori-ashi*, bend right elbow (as if elbow were to touch side of the chest), right palm upward. Bring left hand to forehead, palm upward. While blocking upper level strike with left hand, right hand can enter opponent's crotch. Use both hands to throw opponent.

GLOSSARY

Roman numerals refer to other volumes in this series: I, Comprehensive;
II, Fundamentals; III, Kumite 1; IV Kumite 2; V, Heian, Tekki; VI, Bassai,
Kankū.

ashi: foot, leg

bō uke: blocking stick (attack), 32

chichi: nipple
chūdan: middle level
chūdan choku-zuki: middle level
straight punch, 52, 54, 56, 58,
68, 70, 72, 115, 116; I, 66;
II, 102; IV, 62; V, 28, 126
chūdan kake-uke: middle level
hooking block, 20; I, 61
chūdan mikazuki-geri: middle level
crescent kick, 85; IV, 52, 64;
V, 84, 90; VI, 46, 65
chūdan osae-uke: middle level
pressing block, 17, 19; I, 62, 64;
V, 37, 53, 82, 90; VI, 84
chūdan oshi-age-uke: middle level
upward pressing block, 18, 127,
128, 130, 131
chūdan uchi uke: middle level
block, inside outward, 51, 53, 55,
61, 63, 65, 67, 69, 71; I, 59; II,
22; V, 40; VI, 17, 74
chūdan uke: middle level block,
113, 118, 121, 134, 136; I, 59,
96; II, 90, 106; V, 28; VI, 31, 81
chūdan yoko uchi: middle level side
strike, 21, 22, 23; VI, 124
chūdan-zuki: middle level punch,
77, 83, 86, 119, 120; V, 32; VI,
41, 84

fumidashi: 34; II, 68; V, 58; VI,
65

gasshō uke: block with palm-heels
together, 87
gedan: lower level
gedan barai: downward block, 60
61, 63, 65, 97, 99, 101, 104, 105,

108, 109, 116, 122, 125, 126;
I, 56; II, 106; V, 17; VI, 48, 112
gedan-gamae: lower level posture,
132; IV, 21
gedan ni oshidasu: thrust downward, 133
gedan osae-uke: lower level pressing block, 18, 128, 130, 131
gedan oshidashi: lower level thrust,
34, 36
gedan uchi-barai: lower level
sweeping block, 25
gedan uke: downward block, 37,
38; V, 50; VI, 43, 65, 87, 138,
140
gedan-zuki: lower level punch, 76,
82, 103, 107, 124

hachinoji-dachi: open-leg stance,
98; I, 29; V, 16; VI, 25, 68
hachinoji-dachi shizen-tai: open-
leg stance, natural position, 50
haiwan: upper side of the forearm
heisoku-dachi: informal attention
stance, 16; I, 29; V, 60; VI, 16
hidari: left
hidari ashi-dachi: left leg stance,
35, 74, 112; V, 35; VI, 36, 79
hidari hiza kussu: left knee bent,
104; VI, 30, 76
hidari kōkutsu-dachi: left back
stance, 38, 79, 118; I, 31; II,
52; III, 40; V, 26; VI, 31, 72
hidari mae hangetsu-dachi: left
(leg) in front, half-moon stance,
51; I, 34
hidari mae neko-ashi-dachi: left
(leg) in front cat leg stance, 87;
I, 35; II, 52
hidari sokumen: left side
hidari zenkutsu-dachi: left front
stance, 18, 101, 105; I, 30; II,

18, 52, 141
ippon ken: one-knuckle fist

jōdan: upper level
jōdan age-uke: upper level rising block, 39, 40, 41, 42, 78, 83; I, 57; II, 106
jōdan age-zuki: upper level rising punch, 102, 106, 117, 123; I, 70
jōdan jūji uke: upper level X block, 24; I, 64; V, 64, 74, 80, 90
jōdan kakiwake uke: upper level reverse wedge block, 26; I, 64; V, 68, 74, 76
jōdan oshidashi: upper level thrust, 34, 36
jōdan tsukami-uke: upper level grasping block, 133; V, 115; VI, 35, 64
jōdan uchi uke: upper level block, inside outward, 37, 38; VI, 43, 87
jōdan uke: upper level block, 31; I, 57; II, 106; V, 46; VI, 72
jōdan yoko uchi-barai: upper level side-sweeping block, 27, 28, 29

kakiwake orosu: downward thrust, 30
kamae: posture, 16, 31, 59, 97, 98; III, 14; IV, 40; V, 32; VI, 12, 25, 65, 72
kamaeru: take a posture
kata: shoulder
ken: fist
kiba-dachi: straddle-leg stance, 20, 100; I, 32; II, 52; V, 54; VI, 44, 122
kime: 11, 60; I, 50; III, 15; IV, 118; V, 61
kokō: tiger mouth (shape of hand), 32
koshi: hip

mae: front, in front of
mae keage: front snap kick, 75, 81; I, 86; II, 88, III, 67, 98; V, 41; 46, 48, 69, 75
migi: right
migi ashi-dachi: right leg stance, 33, 75, 103; V, 66; VI, 17, 94
migi ashi mae kōsa-dachi: right leg in front crossed-feet stance, 25; II, 52; V, 68; VI, 138
migi ashi orishiku: right leg kneeling, 97
migi hiza kussu: right knee bent, 99; VI, 30, 78

migi kōkutsu-dachi: right back stance, 37, 73, 119; I, 31; II, 52; III, 40; V, 26; VI, 31, 72
migi mae hangetsu-dachi: right (leg) in front, half-moon stance, 53; I, 34
migi mae hiza kussu: right front knee bent, 133
migi sokumen: right side
migi zenkutsu-dachi: right front stance, 17, 128; I, 30; II, 18, 52; V, 17; VI, 18, 89
mizu-nagare kamae: water flowing position, 100; I, 104; II, 90; IV, 122; V, 78, 90
mune: chest

naname: diagonally
naore: return to *yōi*

ryō: both
ryō ken: both fists
ryō soku: both sides

shizen-tai: natural position, 43, 88, 96; I, 28; V, 16, VI, 16, 68, 131
shō: (open) hand, palm
shō tekubi: hand (and) wrist
shutō: sword hand
sokutō: sword foot

tai soku ni: to the side of the body
tate mawashi-uchi: vertical strike, 73, 79, 84; I, 75; II, 129; V, 18; VI, 106, 138, 139
tate shutō: vertical sword hand
teishō: palm-heel
tekubi: wrist
tsukami-uke: grasping block, 62, 64, 66; V, 115, VI, 35, 64

uchiate: strike
ude: arm
ue: above
uhai tekubi: back of right wrist, 17
uraken: back-fist

waki: side of the chest

yama-gamae: mountain posture, 26, 59
yōi: readiness, 16, 43, 50, 88, 96, 137; II, 70; III, 100; V, 60; VI, 41, 124
yori-ashi: sliding the feet, 20, 25, 26, 34, 36, 69, 71, 141; II, 70; III, 100; V, 60; VI, 41, 124

zempō: front direction